The Problems With Women

By

Bobby Black

The Problems With Women

By

Bobby Black

theproblemswithwomen.com

Published By **OMG BOOKS LIMITED**

ISBN-13: 978-0-9934801-0-2

ISBN-10: 0993480101

Dedication

This book is dedicated to all the men frustrated with the women that have frequented their lives. It's also dedicated to all the women that are going through the lifelong journey of improving themselves.

Contents

Acknowledgements

My 1st acknowledgement must go to Nathan Miller, author of Impressing Employers, for inspiring me and showing me it can be done.

My next acknowledgment must go to Hoda Rizk, who kindly created the eye-catching cover to my specification. Sorry for being a pain.

I cannot forget the help of my Copy Editor D.A.J.C. who with her insights helped the book to have a decisive cutting-edge. She also wrote the blurb alongside her mother, whom I must thank as well.

Introduction

We're living in an age where most of us know exactly what we want and we all want it now. That's usually fine if you have enough funds to buy the material things in life, but when it comes to finding that significant other it becomes harder to find the person of our desires.

This book is about my own personal journey, including accounts from friends, family and observations from the media and our society today.

Being a young man myself, I have an image in my mind of my ideal woman. In short, she's a whore in the bedroom (exclusively for me), a mother in the house, a lady in public and the best friend I could ever have. A part of me knows that I need to keep on dreaming, clearly this woman doesn't exist outside of my mind or she's already been captured by some other lucky bugger.

I can't seem to find her anywhere. I have encountered many women in my life, and although I realise no-one is perfect, nearly every woman I do come across has some sort of defect, problem or issue.

That's what this book is about.

The problems with women.

Not just from my own opinion, but from those of other men and women alike.

I can hear many of your thoughts while you're reading this. A lot of guys are thinking "I know exactly what you're talking about" and can empathise with my dilemma. While many women are thinking "what an 'effing cheek! Men are far from perfect themselves!"

What gives me the right to say such outrageous things?

Free will.

I'm not inciting violence against women and the last time I checked, I still have freedom of speech. To tell you the truth, I've been around the block a few times, having started at a young age. I've had one night stands; short term; medium term and long term relationships.

Let me define those for you:

- One night stand = 1 night
- Short term = Under 2 years
- Medium term = 2 to under 5 years
- Long term = 5 years plus

I've lived with partners and have come close to marriage, although until I find the right woman, that won't happen. I've also had many discussions with a variety of friends and family members, both male and female, about their problems with women. I've even been a mediator for my ex-girlfriend and her partner.

I don't believe men are better than women or vice versa. We are simply different. The truth is I love women. The only problem is, I can't seem to live with them and I can't seem to live without them. It's an eternal paradox. I'm sure plenty of you women feel exactly the same about men.

I'm certain loads of women would like to know what men really think. Not the fake glossed over version that men tell them because they're afraid to speak their mind. No, this is the real nitty gritty version that men only share with their mates in private when nobody's listening or keep to themselves in today's politically correct society. People like to know the truth, and deserve to know it, however painful it might be.

This book pushes across those boundaries and gives an inside view of the way men actually think. It is a fun book that may save a few relationships if the right women read it with an open mind.

It may open the eyes of some of the younger men who might think they know it all when in fact they don't know much. It could give them an insight into what's in stall for them and help them avoid some dodgy women, saving them a lot of heartache.

This book will provide many with situations and stories about women that they can relate to. Some will wet themselves laughing, while others will be fuming with anger as unfortunately the truth usually hurts.

Hopefully it informs, entertains and educates men and women alike.

Happy reading.

Bobby Black

Equality Street

I don't bleed from my genitals once a month every month.

I'm not rubbing in the fact that women do. I'm just making an example to show that we are different. Men don't develop breasts, unless they're fat and grow man boobs. Women don't have penises unless they decide to become transgender. Naturally, we are born with different physical features.

We can't treat everyone the same as not everyone is the same. We don't treat children like adults because they are children, their minds are yet to develop in the way that an adult's has, as they have had less experience in life.

They are different.

Some of us offer our seats to older people because their bodies might need it more than ours. Again, that's because they are different.

Equal, but different.

Gentlemen open doors for women and let them go first. We treat them a little bit gentler than we would our male friends as they are the fairer sex. We offer to pay for dates, if you're old fashioned (or just a gentleman in my opinion), because that's what men do.

I'm not saying women aren't capable of opening doors or paying for dates. I'm just saying that's how men treat women.

We treat them like they are women.

I understand some people go Dutch on dates nowadays, but traditionally, that's not the norm.

We have these feminist who shout out for equal rights and there's nothing wrong with that. But women must not forget what they are, female. Thinking like a lady, but acting like a man when you are clearly not, can lead to disaster. Women have different hormones to men, which leads to them feeling certain emotions on an entirely different scale than their male counterparts.

It's not sexist, it's they're genetical make-up.

We are who we are.

We are equal, but we are different.

We're not just physically different. We are chemically different. Our brain's function differently. I can't multitask to save my life, but most women can. A woman attempting to be hard as nails might have difficulties dealing with the emotional side of that whereas many men won't.

Also, where's the attraction in that?

I like a woman to be warm; soft and gentle not cold; hard and brutal.

Opposites attract and opposites work well together.

Ying and yang, positive and negative, on and off and if you're an IT geek zeros and ones. Even in many same sex relationships, you can tell one person wears the pants and the other one wears the knickers.

Many women like a man that is handsome, strong and confident. A man that takes the lead. Not a wimp who can't make up his mind on where they are going for a date. They'll feel like the vultures in Jungle Book repeating the same repertoire: "What are we gonna do?" "I don't know, what do you wanna do?"

They want the type of guy that makes them feel secure and well looked after and as many women can't make up their minds, it also gives them comfort in knowing that they'll be heading in the right direction, as the guy will make the correct choice for both of them.

My preference in a woman - and many men's preference - is for a woman to be womanly. A woman that is warm in character. That's loving, considerate and affectionate. A woman that takes care of her appearance, but doesn't take all year getting ready.

A woman that's domesticated.

I'm not saying that a woman should be stuck in the house doing all the housework and that she shouldn't be able to have a job and earn a living. And, I'm sure some women would love that role, are already living it, and feel comfortable and secure with their lives. But I like a woman that can help by being able to take care of the household.

There isn't necessarily a right or wrong, it's what works for the individuals in question.

Personally, I don't like women that act like men, and speaking with my cousin, I realised I wasn't alone in that. They act tough and aggressive and have sharp tongues. The way they speak is manly. The way they act is manly. The problem is, deep down inside, the way they feel is womanly.

The words they throw in a man's direction may easily bounce off, as men tend not to take them too seriously. If, on the other hand, a man retaliates and attacks a woman verbally with the same ferociousness, those words can have a long lasting effect on a woman.

Why? Because we are different.

Equal, but different.

The Ideal Woman

For a long time I've been looking for the ideal woman to no avail. I can't seem to find her anywhere.

Does she exist?

Who knows?

My impression of an ideal woman has changed over time. When I was young and foolish my ideal woman consisted of a pretty face, big tits with a nice body.

I didn't even put much thought into what the personality of my potential partner would be like. Not much has changed on the physical side of things, but now, that ideal has developed through my different encounters with women and seeing other men's skirmishes with the opposite sex over the years.

As I said in the introduction, in a nutshell, she's a whore in the bedroom, a mother in the house, a lady in public and a really good friend. In reality she's slightly more complex than that.

For starters, she has to look attractive to me.

Nice eyes. You know those dreamy, seductive

eyes that make your heart melt. And, succulent, juicy lips that make you want to kiss them.

Her face should be stunningly beautiful, although that's just my ideal. A woman doesn't necessarily have to be drop dead gorgeous to be attractive. There are many women out there who don't fit that criteria, but still capture my attention and attract my desires.

I like women with a well-proportioned face not one where her eyes or features are 10 miles apart or merging into one. High cheek bones are also attractive to me, but they are not essential and some women's high cheek bones are too sharp and subtract from her feminine beauty.

Speaking of feminine beauty, I find that natural looks surpass those achieved through cosmetics. I prefer a woman who wears little to no make-up. Some women plaster themselves with make-up and end up looking like clowns.

Have you ever looked at a woman and seen that her face is one colour and her neck is another?

It looks awful.

Worse than that is when you meet a woman, say in a club, where the lighting isn't great. Then, you meet her again in good lighting and she still doesn't look too bad.

Eventually you will see her without the waxworks and you realise she looks terrible. That's usually after you've spent a few quid, time and effort on some dates and you still might have not made it to 4th base (sexual intercourse).

The metamorphic powers of makeup have even apparently led to an Algerian man suing his wife on the first day as a married couple due to him seeing her without makeup for the first time. He's suing her for fraud and psychological damage.

I like a woman who looks attractive without make-up, and so do most men.

We understand the importance of grooming yourself, but sometimes it goes too far.

What is it with shaving off your eyebrows and then penning them in? Have you ever seen these women in the interim between the creation of their drawn brows?

They look totally weird.

In fact they look scary.

I just don't get it.

However, I do get boobs. Big firm tits are a winner. But big tits alone are not enough. If they're sagging down near her knees, that's severely off-putting. I'd prefer a girl with double a's over double g's that droop down to her waist when she takes her bra off.

Also, a nice big round bum is another one of my ideal qualities. Not too big, but the shape of it is important, again firmness is the key.

All of this has to fit on a small to medium frame. From a UK size 8-12 ideally, although there is no strict rule on her clothing size. Women that are too underweight make me feel like I might break them when we get busy in the bedroom.

Some of these catwalk models look like stick insects.

And, this isn't a crusade to belittle any woman of any body type, yet I must express my opinion.

I really fail to see how a grown man that isn't a paedophile, can find their bodies attractive. Many of them look like skin and bones. Their bones actually look like they're gonna pierce and break through their skin.

Women that are too overweight are not my cup of tea either. Especially excessively overweight women with humongous rolls of fat. And, I've found that sometimes, some of them smell disgustingly unpleasant. I'm sure they have their fans, but I'm not one of them.

I know some women have weight issues because of thyroid problems or the medication they're taking etc. and so they cannot control how much they weigh, and as said before, there are guys who prefer bigger women, and smaller ones alike.

But I am not jumping at the chance to be with them. Everybody has their type and mine doesn't extend certain body types. Especially muscular women, who resemble Arnold Schwarzenegger in his prime.

Height, race, and age are not really important to me, although I don't want a woman that's taller than me, including when she wears heels, if indeed she does wear them.

Beauty shows itself in many forms, I wouldn't say I have a type as there are too many variances in beauty for me to narrowly define to one set of traits. Saying that there are some traits that stand out more than others, as mentioned above.

I am perfectly aware that you can't put a

price on a good personality, looks are only part of the bargain. Like Hovis, I am searching for the best of both worlds, good looks and a beautiful character.

Nothing can beat a beautiful character. A person's character can win you over and melt your heart. At the centre of a person's character is their mindset, the way they think. Someone's mindset determines how they behave and what they do.

A person with terminal negativity is a right put-off. Nothing is possible in their mind, a lot of the time they don't even bother trying. I believe these people attract the negative things which seem to frequent their lives regularly.

I'm not into religious fanatics either.

Don't get me wrong, I don't mind if a woman is religious, but if she's knocking on people's doors or handing out flyers like a drug dealer on the side of the road, trying to convert them to join her on her religious escapade, then she's not the one for me.

I'm sure there's plenty more constructive things she could be doing with her time, like spending it with me.

What truly makes a woman ideal are the little

things about her entire makeup. A woman that takes care of her appearance, down to wearing matching sexy underwear. A woman that loves sex as much as I do. A woman that knows how to look after her man, and can hold a good conversation. A woman that isn't that interested in my bank balance. A woman that's loyal. A woman that is intellectual, but not arrogant with her knowledge.

A woman that can give you space when you need it and not feel insecure because you're out of her company for 5 minutes. These are some of the characteristics that a lot of men crave for, myself included.

A woman's attitude determines how she will approach things. For example, you have women that can but won't cook because they have, what I would call, 'the wrong attitude'. Then, you'll have a woman who is clearly terrible in the kitchen, but she's willing to learn and practice.

She might poison you or burn down the house in the process, but at least she's willing to try and learn how to cook.

It's a well-known saying that a way to a man's heart is through his stomach, and I can't deny that a woman who's a good cook, and is also a willing one, is a joy to any man. Problem is, a lot of the women who can cook well, are overweight.

I've already told you about them.

Funnily enough, one of the most important things about finding a woman is not necessarily about the woman herself.

It's about chemistry.

You know when you click with somebody and everything just feels right. Even when silence pops its head up it's not uncomfortable, in fact everything feels quite natural. The conversation flows, you get each other's jokes and there's this mutual attraction that burns inside and glows through the eyes. Something you can't hide or fake. You both seem to have things in common.

When you find that person who makes you feel good inside and you them; that's when those coveted memorable moments arise and you begin to feel that the relationship is going to be something worthwhile.

That's what I'm looking for.

If there's no chemistry, there's no future.

Beauty & The Beast

Let's start with beauty.

She's stunningly beautiful. Absolutely drop dead gorgeous, she's practically glowing with radiance. As a man, your heart melts when you see her. Even other women find her attractive.

However, there's a problem with the archetype of beautiful women that are nice and know it, and it's blatantly obvious that they know it.

They walk around like their shit don't stink.

They're snooty, arrogant and totally unapproachable. These women want you to bleed before you can even get their number. You'll have to be extremely charming, funny, well dressed and well-kept if you're to get a positive response from them.

Go ahead, try approaching them and see what happens.

Their hard exterior may be a defence mechanism, to shield them from being hurt or hide previous pain, regardless of their motives, their response is usually so unnecessarily blasé. You'll be talking to them and they act as if you don't exist and that's if they're even paying any attention to you at all.

I'm not saying that if a woman isn't interested in a bloke she should still be overly welcoming to all strange men approaching her but that's not the issue here. There are many ways to let a man down, but it would seem these women don't like the gentle approach. This is a serious attitude problem that needs fixing.

I'm not saying women shouldn't have confidence either, but whatever happened to humbleness with this wild breed of female. They most probably wonder why so few men approach them.

Then, there are beautiful women that need to take a look in the personality mirror.

They are Bitches with a capital B.

Some of them don't even seem to know how to be nice. Their looks could win them Miss World but the way they handle themselves is far from beautiful. But the most puzzling thing is that some of the women who behave this way don't always fall into the good looks category. Some of them are ugly on the outside too.

In life I believe it's nice to be important, but it's even more important to be nice. Being nice is free. It doesn't cost a penny. So why be horrible?

I know some may think I myself am being mean by saying some controversial things, but don't confuse my unabridged honesty with hypocrisy. These thoughts aren't exclusive to me, most people just wouldn't dream of saying them out loud, for fear of being persecuted.

These women go out of their way to be nasty, while at the same time being nasty seems to come naturally to them. They don't smile much and if they do, it's usually an evil Cruella type smile because they've just done something devilish and they're relishing in their sinful glory.

They're downright rude.

Some of these women seem to fit into the: I'm nice and I know it category too.

The worst thing about these women is that they can blind you with their beauty, and further this false representation of their character by wooing you with their charisma skills as well. They draw you into the comfort zone and then you lower your guard. Then, they strike like a lioness, pouncing on her prey from her tall, dry sand-coloured grass camouflage. At a moment's notice; she's sinking her sharp teeth deep into its raw flesh.

You feel sucker punched and it hurts because you totally wasn't expecting it which disorientates you.

Sometimes there's telltale signs, which, if you can spot, could save you drama if you abandon ship. Usually they are not naturally charming, so if you sense that she's not the genuine article you're most probably right. Our instincts are usually right, so steer clear of these women if you can and NEVER fall in love with one.

She'll eat you for breakfast. Not sexually, literally.

My other gripe is with beautiful women who think they are ugly. They are the opposite of women who are obnoxious with their beauty. It's ok if it happens now and again, but if it's an ongoing occurrence then it can become annoying.

We all know that a lot of women like a little bit of reassurance from time to time. But these women seem to rely on other people's compliments, and put themselves down at every available chance.

There's a delicate balance that needs to be achieved between over confidence and the complete lack of self-esteem. It comes across as a desperate need of acceptance, and that they are looking for you to tell them how beautiful they are or tell them that they're not fat etc.

After you facilitate that they still don't believe you.

Other women compliment them on their good looks. Guys hound them on the street, throwing all sorts of praise and compliments in their direction. Yet, these women are convinced they are the ugly duckling. Other than reassuring these women to no avail, there's not much else you can do to help them.

It's a personal problem that they need to deal with and overcome.

These women are likely to think you want to sleep with every other woman and their dogs because they all look better than her, in her opinion. She'll even accuse you of trying to flirt with her mother if you have a friendly relationship with her; and when I say relationship, I mean strictly platonic.

Now that we've dealt with the 'beauty' in this chapter's title; let's deal with the beasts. The beast that believes she's God's gift to men. I know they say beauty is in the eye of the beholder, but some women are clearly a lot less attractive than others.

Let's be honest, they're ugly.

It's not their fault, they were born that way.

If you're ugly I believe you should accept it.

We all have different pros and cons about us, if you're unfortunate enough to be hard to look at just take it on the chin. That doesn't mean that you should wallow in self-pity. Just accept it and get on with your life. Focus on some of your other traits so you're a nicer person to be around.

But there are a few women who refuse to accept their looks.

They look at themselves with rose tinted glasses, but they need to take a trip to Spec Savers. I think some of them get encouraged by social media, leading to them becoming severely arrogant. Thanks to the advances of technology, we now have; Photoshop, Instagram and other sorts of tech that can make you look better than you really are, are often overused.

Guys may see the make-believe version of a

woman online and give them the most flattering comments on their beauty. Other guys are desperate enough that they don't care what a women looks like, they just want to get their willies wet.

They'll give these women glowing compliments all day long. Boosting these women's self-esteem to unjustifiable levels so that they actually believe that they are gloriously beautiful. They may even get compliments offline, increasing their egos further. Some men aren't bothered what women look like, but they know the right things to say to get into their hearts and minds and make them drop their knickers.

In my opinion, these types of men are akin to serious sexual predators, worthy of being headhunted by the army.

If getting into the hearts and minds of people was a skill, then these guys are experts. The unfortunate fact of the matter is that these women are like the burgers in 'Falling Down', they don't resemble their pictures online and in real life, they are a disappointment.

This situation seems to have a negative effect on these women because now they think they're stunning and they're not. If you're ugly, I would advise you to have a stunning personality to compensate for your lack of external beauty.

That doesn't seem to be the case with many of these ugly women. I personally believe regardless of your looks, personality gets you a long way in life.

There's no need to be a bitch just for the sake of it.

Women & Their Bodies

I actually believe that a large proportion of women suffer from body dysmorphia, which is a disorder in which a person believes their physical appearance to be grossly diverse from what it actually is to the outside world. No matter a women's weight, they attach their own belief as to whether they are beautiful or not. When they look in the mirror, they see something different from the truth.

Slim women think they are fat. Some of these women aren't even slim they're so skinny they look like twiglets that might snap if you hug them too hard.

I once had a circle of female friends that loved when I was around because every time I saw them, I'd criticise them about how skinny they looked. They saw this as a compliment and they loved it.

In fact, I was being serious and used to tell them that they looked malnourished and anorexic. Their faces would turn into smiles and they'd thank me for the compliment I wasn't giving them.

Personally, I like women with a little bit of meat on them, not just skin and bones.

Next up you have the women that are obviously fat, but think they are skinny, not slim, but skinny.

There's fat everywhere, but in their mind they're underweight even if the mirror, the scales and their clothes all tell them otherwise. Friends, family and even strangers in the street echo the same thing, but it all falls on deaf ears. As far as these women are concerned, they are skinny, anorexic even.

Some of these women are clearly obese.

In my opinion, some form of intervention needs to happen with the women mentioned above. They either need an appointment at the opticians or some severe form of mind training or therapy. Evidently something is wrong with these women's perspectives of themselves.

I'm actually convinced that the majority of women have a problem with some part of their body. That doesn't necessarily mean body dysmorphia, but there is a sense of insanity in the way that certain women behave.

For some reason a lot of women don't like their bodies or a part of their body. If their boobs are bigger than average, then they're too big and they need a reduction. If they're average size or smaller they're too small and they want them bigger.

It's not just boobs, its bums, tums and everything else. Maybe the nose they were born with isn't quite how they like it or their lips are too thin or too thick. For others, it's their bingo wings, their feet or their hands. They just feel uncomfortable in their own skin.

They can't just accept who they are and be happy. And, this is true for many people, not just women.

The problem lies in the fact that these women constantly go on about it.

They ask you the same question they asked yesterday as if they expect you to see a difference one day later. "Do you think I've put on weight?" How the hell am I supposed to tell without pushing you onto the scales and weighing you from one day to the next?

I'm sure most people's bodies don't put on or lose weight that drastically from one day to the next. If I'm in regular close contact with you I'm hardly going to notice am I?

Most women are constantly battling with the way they look, when in the end, that's just how they were made to look, meant to look even.

I'm me. I was born the way I am. If some people consider me ugly I just have to live with it and accept it. Others may find me extremely handsome. The fact is your face is your face and I believe you should learn to like it and if you think you're totally unattractive, work on that personality of yours.

As for your body, if you're unhappy with your weight, do something about it.

If you're overweight go to the gym and eat less. If you're underweight eat a little bit more. I suggest that you believe the scales when they tell you your weight or go to the doctor to clarify the healthy weight for your age and height etc. Also, eat healthy and consult a dietitian if you're unsure.

Unless you're severely under or overweight, don't worry so much.

Be healthy, eat healthy, exercise and make sure you're nice to other people. And, stop asking the same or similar questions every day or every week.

Life isn't all about what your stomach looks like in the mirror.

Hair We Go Again

Women and their hair.

They waste half of their life waiting at the hairdressers and then spend a generation getting their hair done once they are finally attended to. All in all, they spend fortunes doing their hair, in time and money.

If they saved up the money they spent on their hair, I'm sure within a short space of time they could go on a decent holiday. I'm not saying women can't afford to go on holiday - as plenty of them can - but they could save a lot more money if they spent less on their hair.

The worst part of it all, a lot of women spend a large percent of their income on their hair and it doesn't even look good. Why these women spend an arm and a leg on hairstyles that often don't suit them or, worse than that, look hideous is a mystery to me.

A woman will have nice long, flowing hair which she can put into many different styles, only to chop it off. After the novelty of short hair has worn off, these women complain about not having long hair.

They'll talk to their friends and say stuff like I

wish I had long hair like you. Their friends are usually too polite to tell them that they shouldn't have cut their hair off in the first place.

In my opinion, and I mean no offence when I say this, but I find that women with really short hair look like they're suffering with either alopecia or cancer or they look like they're a lesbian. I have nothing against lesbians and I'm not saying all lesbians have short hair.

When I see a woman with hair as short as mine or shorter (my hair is quite low) then I usually tend to think she's a lesbian. Maybe I'm wrong for thinking that, but that's what it looks like to me. And, perhaps I'm not alone in this way of thinking. If these women are looking for a man and wondering why no-one is courting them that could be the reason.

Another thing that strikes me as illogical is women that cut off their hair only to replace it with false hair. That doesn't make any sense to me whatsoever. If you have nice long hair, then you cut it off, I'd assume that you want short hair. Why on earth would you then go and spend more money on fake hair?

In a lot of cases fake hair looks fake, and this little fact distorts a woman's entire image.

Women don't even seem to realise, they think it looks great. Their friends don't do them any favours, they will all praise each other on how nice their hair looks even if they think it looks terrible.

Most women rarely tell the truth if they're asked by someone what they look like. For some reason they like to tell a nice big fat white lie, although there's nothing nice about it.

If a woman has fake hair and other women can't tell that it's fake, then that's a sign that her hair truly does look good. But if a woman has fake hair and most men can tell its fake then they need to get their money back.

Better still, they should just wear their own hair, there's nothing wrong with that. If it needs styling go and wait half a year until it's your turn in the queue and get it styled. It's much better than the fake stuff, believe me.

A lot of women wear fake hair to avoid the daily hassle of styling their hair in the mornings.

They're lazy.

Rather than do their hair in the mornings, they buy fake hair. Fake hair that looks a lot worse than their real hair. They just can't be bothered. Or they know that they take all year to get ready and so they opt for a shortcut, when in fact doing their hair will make it 2 years instead of 1.

A lot of women treat their hair like it's the US dollar in Zimbabwe. If you look like you're thinking about touching it, they go into some hysterics.

It's an unwritten rule. Never touch a woman's hair unless she gives you permission. Men like to run their fingers through a woman's hair or hold it while being intimate. Some women react as if you just started troubling the wrong hole and have a fit.

Relax, it's only hair, don't panic.

I'm sure you have a mirror in your purse to fix it back just the way you like it.

Speak Your Mind

As you can probably tell by now, I'm not afraid to speak my mind. I say it like it is.

Nowadays we live in a politically correct society where people are publicly condemned for having an opinion. Just because your opinion doesn't flow with the status quo, doesn't mean that you should be prohibited from expressing yourself freely.

If we're not careful we'll drift into a society where the mind police will be out to get us. George Orwell's 1984 was a warning of where not to go in terms of society, not subtle advice of what our society should be heading towards.

A lot of people are scared to talk the truth for whatever reasons. With the advent of social media, the younger generations are used to typing what's on their mind much more than speaking it. Many of them seem out of their depth in face to face or voice to voice situations, with many terrified of any confrontation altogether.

Many people aren't just afraid to speak their mind for fear of public reprisals – they're afraid to publicly agree with an opinion that doesn't flow with the perceived moral high ground at a particular moment in time.

People's views can change. Up until recently, while writing this book, there was public outcry at immigrants fleeing war torn countries, such as Syria, to seek refuge and safety on the shores of Europe, in hopes of a better life.

People were dead against it.

Then, a picture of a dead child on a beach emerged.

Many have since changed their tune, after all we are all human regardless of where we were born.

The point is, you shouldn't be afraid to speak your mind or stand up for someone's viewpoint if you agree with it.

Women, in general, over the course of my lifetime at least, tend to speak a lot. The problem is they often say a lot, but not what they really mean, but they expect you to translate their beating around the bush into clear English which can be easily understood.

Don't get me wrong, some women wear their heart on their sleeves and express themselves clearly. There's no mistaking what these women say as they say what they have to say nice and blunt, a lot of the time too blunt for my liking, but at least you get what they're saying and there's no ambiguity.

Women that speak their mind are a minority and they're on the decline.

As a man I know we're different than women, but some things are seriously frustrating and hard to understand.

A man will be in a relationship with a woman and everything will be hunky dory, well at least that's what a man may think. Little does he know that he's done something that's annoyed, frustrated or upset his significant other.

She may not do or say anything at all and just act as if everything is normal. But, despite her exterior demeanour, inside she's expecting you to read her mind and know what you've done wrong. Yes, she expects you to be psychic and know exactly what you've done that's upset her. If you don't, she'll be even more pissed with you.

Now a woman may do a number of things to let you know that you've slipped up in some shape or form.

If you're lucky enough, you might be with one of the women that does something to let you know you're in her bad books. She might give you the subtlest of hints and expect you to notice it and decipher it and address whatever it is you've done to offend her. Other women might give you the silent treatment, while others will give you the no sex treatment.

Now, what if you were to ask them what's wrong? She most probably will respond by saying; "nothing". As a man, a lot of us will take this at face value. She said nothing's wrong so everything must be fine, maybe she's just in a quiet state or she's just not in the mood for sex.

The truth of the matter is, she is pissed, but she's not speaking her mind.

I once was going through a time in my life where my schedule was quite hectic. When I spoke to the women I was seeing, it was usually over the phone; having long, deep meaningful conversations. Since I knew I would be busy I let her know, explaining that I wouldn't be able to talk to her for a while, but I'd contact her afterwards.

She was really understanding and supportive at the time, or so I thought. She told me to take my time and not to worry about her. I was well impressed as I knew that she could be quite possessive over the time I didn't spend with her.

When my busy schedule finished I contacted her and was surprised to hear snide remarks under her breath alongside bitterness in her tone and negative sarcasm related to my absence.

She clearly wasn't happy with my busy schedule and my absence from speaking to her, even though I had explained the situation and I did ensure to message her from time to time in that period, to make sure she knew I hadn't forgotten her.

Why didn't she just say something at the time instead of pretending to be understanding and supportive?

Instead, she lied and led me to believe everything was cool when it wasn't, which altered my behaviour. I used the time to do the things that I needed to do. Otherwise, I may have sacrificed that a little to comfort her as I cared about her feelings.

Why did she not say anything?

Because many women can't speak their bloody minds and they expect you to just know what they're thinking like your name's Yoda or David Blaine.

Guess what ladies?

If you spoke your mind, we'd understand you better and act accordingly. So quit with the riddles or the silent treatment and speak your mind, tactfully.

Make it nice and sugar coated if it's negative.

Women who speak their mind can tend to be abrupt - like this book, but that isn't going to go down well with most guys. We like women because they're warm, soft and gentle. We don't want aggressive, masculine and brutal women, traditionally that's not our impression of women.

It's not what we want and it's not what we're used to.

Make Up Your Mind

Left or right?

Or possibly straight ahead?

Or maybe you should just make up your bloody mind! What is with women and indecisiveness? Can't you just decide and go with it? It's annoying at best and infuriating at the worst.

A lot of women, not all women, but a lot of them, can't seem to decide on anything without hours of deliberating. Why is that? I don't understand it.

I understand that people in general like to double check things they're unsure about with a friend, spouse, family member or even an expert in the field concerned. But I don't get why some women can't make any decisions for themselves.

You can't be uncertain about everything.

I like to get things right and I often clarify things with people, including them on the decision making process. But this is usually exclusive to an event where I am doing something on behalf of another person and would like to know exactly what they want and how they want it. It's an external matter.

When it is something internal I don't have any problem deciding things for myself.

These women can't decide whether to go out or stay in, what to wear if they do go out, whether to buy something new or put something on that they haven't worn for a while around a particular set of people, or even how they should do their hair; this way or that?

The list of things goes on and on.

If they have a problem at work and there are guidelines, rules and procedures to follow, they still can't make up their mind about things. Should they ask the manager or someone else? It baffles me as to how many questions must be buzzing around in these women's heads?

If you're unfortunate enough to be that woman's partner, may God help you.

They'll explain scenarios to you all day every day and expect you to come up with the magical solutions. You might feel appreciated in the beginning because she's coming to you and she respects your opinion enough to ask you.

That might be a nice little ego boost when you're starting out. But over time, when she fails to grow more independent and start to make decisions for herself, it can become frustrating. Especially when you're busy doing other stuff and she's calling your phone like it's an emergency only to ask you what should she say to her friend or something else trivial.

Really?

I'm busy. Make up your own mind. See what happens.

Worst of all, if things don't turn out right, they'll blame the person who gave them the advice. It's actually not that person's fault, they were only trying to help per your request.

It's your fault for not making up your own mind. Everyone in the world should take responsibility for their actions, and decide for themselves. If all goes wrong learn from the experience and make a better decision next time, thus growing. It's how we learn and develop as individuals.

Unfortunately, some refuse to make any decisions at all and live in a state of limbo. Doing barely anything with their lives unless they get advice from someone else or are literally told and ordered what to do by others.

Obviously they must get some sort of comfort or satisfaction from that, otherwise they would fix up and start living, not just leaching off other people's ideas, but doing things through their own decision making.

Some men actually love this type of woman. Why? Because they are control freaks and now they can control every little aspect of her life and she'll willingly abide by his commands.

These women become so dependent on that man that if they break up for any reason she'll feel like she's in the Sahara desert without a camel.

She'll be totally lost.

She won't know what to do.

That's why she'll most probably stick with him for as long as possible because her life depends on his decisions. It's not a good look.

I know they say if you're unsure about something, ask. Fair enough. But you can't be unsure about every bloody thing. Well, obviously you can, at the detriment of your own personality.

I think this goes deeper into self-belief. These women lack confidence in themselves. They question whether they are right or wrong all the time because they don't believe in their own ability to get things right.

Take responsibility and deal with the consequences. I can't say this enough. Eventually you'll start to make better decisions and have more confidence in yourself. It takes time, but practice makes perfect.

Old Vs The Young

I used to see a young lady and once, I asked her if she could cook. She told me that she could. So, I then asked her; "what can you cook?" She said she could cook toast, eggs and beans.

I looked at her.

I waited.

There was no smile.

She was dead serious.

I asked her if there was anything else she could cook, but that was about it.

There was nothing else.

Was she so ignorant to think that sticking bread in the toaster, beans in the microwave and boiling eggs in a pan - that in my experience have no chance of burning - amounted to cooking?

That's one of the problems with some younger women nowadays. They are not domesticated (and this goes for a lot of men, regardless of age I'm afraid). A lot of them don't know how to cook, wash themselves, clean and tidy their living quarters or iron a few pieces of garments.

Traditionally, women are the cornerstone of the house.

They make everything run smoothly. They clean the house from top to bottom. They make the meals, at least three times a day. They look after the children - and their children's friends when they come over - and a wealth of other things. In all honesty, they deserve medals for their input into the family home.

In modern times, things have progressed and men contribute their fair share too, as is expected. Due to the financially difficult times we are living in, sometimes it's not plausible for one partner to stay at home and the other being the bread winner. Two people need to contribute for many couples to stay afloat financially.

I personally believe men and women alike should have at least the basic household skills. A lot of the younger women, and men, resort to begging others to fulfil their daily needs. Some of them actually can wash, cook and clean, etc. but refuse to.

Do you remember the show 'Can't Cook Won't Cook'? These lazy buggers fall into the: Won't category because: "Why should I?" or "I can't be bothered". Quite frankly, it's disgusting. And, as unfortunate as it may be, that's the direction society is going into.

Many older women have dab old hands in the kitchen, in the whole house in fact. They can rustle a good meal, keep the house spotless, wash and iron clothes, keep themselves in pristine condition and hold several conversations at the same time. They've had so much practice, it's second nature to them.

Some younger women have a glow about them. They're naturally happy and more willing to try and make things work. This obviously goes in their favour. They cause less headache, less arguments and are more willing to go with the flow.

On the whole there's usually less resistance than with an older woman. Speaking as a man this is refreshing and comforting. There's less friction and more tranquillity in a relationship. They still have the ability to fall in love and enjoy the moment.

They're younger. Their view of the world is still untainted. Anything is possible and nothing is impossible.

They smile. They're happy. They're full of life.

Some older women on the other hand, are

bitter and guarded individuals.

It can be hard to create something meaningful with them because they're so closed off and protect themselves in many different ways.

Isn't it better to meet someone new and treat them based on their own merit, not on how past lovers have behaved? If your heart is swaying towards loving them, love them like you have never loved before.

How else is a relationship supposed to be successful?

While a younger woman will open up and give a man's way of thinking a try, many older women won't open up and are not open to looking at things from someone else's perspective. They close their minds off from other suggestions and can turn selfish, but they still expect a relationship to work out.

Now, the concept of a woman adjusting her behaviour in order to benefit a man will understandably anger many female readers. However, this isn't a double standard. I believe that men should do the same.

When you meet someone and enter a relationship you are two different entities. You both have your own beliefs, morals and principles. However, you are two becoming one. You should learn about your partner's likes and dislikes. If you want a relationship to work, both of you should adapt and compromise a little without losing who you are.

These older women have their own ideas and many refuse to deviate from their rigid way of thinking. They bring all this baggage from previous relationships in one form or another and prevent the present relationship from blossoming into something beautiful.

They're hard bloody work.

They've forgotten how to smile and be nice because they cannot let go of the hurt they've endured in past relationships, allowing it to taint the new one.

Take a second to think about it. What type of company do you enjoy being around?

I like to be around people that make me smile, that enjoy a laugh and that are happy. Who wants to be around a miserable old bag?

Not me for certain.

Another belief of mine is, what you think is what you get. If you drive your man away from you, guess what he'll do?

Leave.

These older women have too much baggage.

They've allowed too many men to shit on them.

They won't allow another man access to their heart, unless he is the perfect partner they have conjured in their mind. Even if you're not taking liberties with them, their warped mind deludes them into thinking that you are blatantly taking the piss.

Many may call the younger women naïve, but that's only if the man is taking advantage of her in some shape or form. If a man genuinely cares about her and her welfare, he'll have her best interests in mind. The relationship can blossom and develop into something beautiful.

Well, that's the way it should be, but unfortunately for many younger women they are still to mature. They may still act rather childish at times. This can lead to them being stubborn and spiteful because they're feeling stroppy. Many are yet to understand themselves and their own feelings and so have difficulty emphasising with others.

They don't yet understand life with all its complexities.

An older woman may be more understanding about your time and commitment. She may understand that men need to go out and achieve to make them feel good about themselves. Whereas a younger woman may just want your time and not understand that outside of work you also spend time on a hobby or a business idea.

An older woman may have her own friends and hobbies to occupy her time. A younger one may do also, but love is new to them so they'll yearn for you more. Which is nice, until it becomes suffocating and you don't have time to do the stuff that you want, and need to do.

You might want to hang out with the guys. The younger woman will want to come too, as she may be used to the type of relationship where you're stuck to each other like superglue. It comes with the territory, as that's what some of them do, but it might not be what you have in mind.

The younger woman may also do things that embarrass you.

She's young and is easier to influence by new trends and all sorts. One day, you'll meet up for an outing, and before you've even greeted each other, you'll be staring at the new septum piercing between her nostrils that wasn't there the last time you saw her.

If you're like me, you'll be disgusted. I deeply despise this type of piercing. Why would you choose to look like a male cow? How the fashion trend became popular is beyond me.

Older women tend to be less impulsive, and stick to their own traditions, unless she's still a wild child at heart or going through an identity crisis. Once you get to know an older woman, you should know what to expect. She'll be less likely to float with the wind when new fads come along.

An older woman will be more likely to know how to behave in front of others. They'll have the benefit of having a better sense of perception and understand what's right and what's wrong in your view and act accordingly. A younger woman may be more impulsive and act more on emotions and without much thought.

I've also found that younger women are open to try things in the bedroom. Some older women are also, but in my experience, and the experience of my male peers, the majority won't consider many things they haven't tried before.

That's pretty unfortunate as men love freaks.

If you offer your man a threesome with one of your attractive female friends he'll jump at the chance. Even if she's unattractive, he most probably won't decline. Some might think it's some sort of test and will refuse point blank, but the vast majority will be taking off their pants, eagerly asking when your friend is due over.

Don't believe me?

Get a good looking friend of yours, both of you dress up in sexy lingerie and wait for your man to come home. Kiss each other to let him know you're serious and to prove it's not a test and see what happens. He'll be all over you two like a male member of the public let loose on a couple of pornstars.

It might be rather difficult to stop him to let him know it's not going to happen, as it's a test, once my point has been proven cut it short, unless you don't mind going through with it.

My argument is, women that are wishy-washy in the bedroom will find themselves with a frustrated partner who might just cheat on them or leave them because they're not satisfied. I'm not justifying those that cheat, merely providing understanding.

Younger women tend to be up for new things.

Possibly because they've grown up in an age where porn is easily accessible. The porn that's out there breaks all boundaries. Some of it is revolting to be honest.

Saying that, some older women know a trick or two that will get any man's toes curling.

Younger women can't spend 5 minutes with you without looking at their phone or taking a selfie. They're always checking out who commented or liked a pic. You'll be out at a restaurant and get more conversation from the waiter or the waitress because she'll be messaging or making calls when she should be eating or focussing her attention on you.

What is it with these selfies? Every 5 minutes she'll want to take a picture and ask you to get in it or take it for her. If it's not that, she'll be recording videos for Snapchat. They'll be walking into lampposts recording videos on the go.

Another problem with younger women, is they are more prone to cheat in my opinion. An older woman will appreciate a good relationship and leave if it's not up to scratch. A younger woman is more used to different types of relationships, like friends with benefits, fuck buddies and 'it's complicated' types.

As a man, you might think you're in a relationship with a young woman, and so you devote your time and energy, but in her mind you're not, and it doesn't matter whether she is the same age as you or not, she will still break your heart.

It's just a little bit of fun.

Sorry.

Women & Their Friends

If you're a man and you meet a woman the best thing you can do is get along with her friends, not too much, as the woman may become jealous and start to think that you fancy her friends over her.

The reason I advise men to get along with her friends, is because these friends can be very powerful, especially if the woman you are seeing is indecisive. Even if she's not indecisive they can still wield a great deal of power.

These friends may decide on a number of things and you might be totally oblivious. They may decide on whether a woman will go out with you on a date, on whether she enters a relationship with you to whether she sleeps with you.

Later on down the line, when you're deep in a relationship with this woman, if you two have had an argument, they may decide on whether you sleep in the bed or on the couch. They may influence her to see someone else, they may even provide that someone else and ultimately those friends may decide to end your relationship.

These friends are like the MPs in the cabinet

or the top bosses in the mafia and they can make many decisions in your relationship, deciding whether you sink or swim with the fishes.

When you're messaging a woman, whether by text or some form of social media, little do you know that actually you may be messaging a consortium of her and her friends. They'll be laughing over your message together and deciding as a group or individually what the reply will be.

Other than the obvious reason that you're actually trying to communicate and connect with the woman of your interest, and not the group of women that you're not particularly interested in, there's another problem with this scenario.

In the beginning of relationships, women tend to sing your praises and say all the nice and lovely things about you. As the relationship develops and those nice and lovely things become more commonplace they tend to mention less about your wonderful qualities or the good things that you do. They might not necessarily badmouth you, but they say less about the good stuff.

When something bad or unpleasant occurs, they'll go on about it until the cows come home. Because they haven't said much about you in a positive sense lately your character now evolves, sometimes into a demonic cunt.

Not to say that whatever it was that happened was extremely bad, but because now they tend to only mention the bad stuff about you, their friends are getting a negative perception of you.

Also, because they are not always there when these things happen and women don't always explain every little detail it can sound worse than it really is.

This is when they start to get into your girlfriend's head. Steering her in a direction of hate and resentment. They can turn your lovely, loving girlfriend into a spiteful, bitter bitch.

The power of friends. Men be careful, this is your warning.

My Grandmother always told me "Show me your company and I'll tell you who you are."

Your girlfriend's friend's personalities can rub off on her. They may encourage her to see someone new, even if they haven't heard anything bad about you. They themselves might just be the type to sleep around and they might meet a feller who has a mate for your girlfriend.

It's as easy as that.

They might be the type of person who are not happy in their own lives and secretly don't want to see others happy. They'll encourage your girlfriend to do things that will ruin your relationship.

They might corrupt your girlfriend because they're jealous. Before, when you weren't in the picture, your girlfriend used to spend 'x' amount of time with them. Now you're on the scene they see her a lot less so they decide to sabotage your relationship.

Be careful of the power of friends. I cannot stress this enough. If her friends dislike you for whatever reason, which may not even be justified, your relationship could be doomed, even before its offset.

The next woman to worry about, is the woman with no friends and sometimes little or no family. You may feel like a king when you become the centre of her attention. She may cater to your every need. But it's best that you know you are her everything.

Her whole life will depend on you.

Sounds great.

Wrong.

Unless you have no friends and family and no life of your own, this woman will end up suffocating you to death. Her life will depend upon your decisions. If you upset her it will be your responsibility to lift her mood. Even if you don't upset her, but she's feeling down for whatever reason, it will be your responsibility to make her happy again.

She will call you all the time and bug the life out of you because she has no one else to talk to but you. You won't be able to breathe. If you want to do stuff without her, maybe a lads' night out, she might end up phoning or messaging you all night because she's bored, lonely and missing your company, which may have the knock-on effect of ruining your night out with the lads.

If she asks for your advice and your advice doesn't go so well, it will be your fault. She'll blame you. On the upside, if it goes well you'll also get the credit, but life with this type of woman can be claustrophobic and unhealthy.

Another woman to be wary of, is the woman that doesn't have any female friends, but has a bunch of male friends.

If this girl is half attractive many of these

men will be waiting for a lucky day when they get to have their wicked way with her. Depending on the woman, one or some of these men may have slept with her already. They may still be sleeping with her.

These women will turn around and tell you they don't get along with women because they're too bitchy. That statement in itself should worry you. It's not that women are too bitchy because although some women definitely are bitchy, not all of them are. People like to see themselves as innocent when in fact, a woman making this statement is more than likely to be the bitchy one.

She doesn't get along with women because she's too bitchy.

As it goes, men treat women differently to how they treat men and vice versa.

On the whole we tend to be kinder to the opposite sex. A man will show more of his gentle side to a woman.

Men aren't gentle with each other unless we're going through a difficult time, such as relationship pain, or being diagnosed with a life threatening condition. It's an unwritten rule that we don't even acknowledge in our minds, but we act out in reality.

For example, if a man is in a car accident and he's still alive, his male friend will show his softer side. He might even cry, which most men tend not to do in front of other men, if they cry at all. This is because something out of the ordinary has happened and they might lose a mate, so it's ok to show your more compassionate side. In normal circumstances men are a little bit rough around the edges with other men.

We're softer with women and the more attractive she is, the nicer we are to them.

We know that women are, in general, the fairer sex so we treat them accordingly. Some women notice this difference and tend to surround themselves with male friends. As I mentioned before, these men are waiting for you to slip up so they can be the shoulder to cry on and the emergency willy to lie on.

She most probably won't tell you if she slept with one of these men in the past. So she'll be emotionally connected to this man - as when women have sex they usually, not always and not all women, get an attachment to the man they are being intimate with.

Most women would rather sleep with someone familiar to them than someone unfamiliar to them. This means those male friends of hers are likely to get a chance to sleep with her even if she hasn't in the past and hasn't got any intention of doing so right now.

A big part of why people sleep with each other is because of opportunity.

Men may dream of sleeping with their favourite pornstars, but it's highly unlikely that this will occur due to circumstance. Unless they are in the porn industry or they're willing to pay big bucks, it's not gonna happen.

On the other hand, these male friends may get the opportunity to be in the right place at the right time and get a lucky dip with your girlfriend.

I've warned you.

Some women have so many friends it's unbelievable. With these women, it's hard to get a minute of her time. Now I'm all for women having friends and a good support group; it takes the pressure off of us men.

When she has too many friends to count and she's always busy with them, then there can be a problem. I'm not talking about social media friends and followers where the vast majority she most probably doesn't even know them personally.

It's perfectly fine if you're not in a serious relationship, but if she can't make time for you because she's always busy with others, and you're in what could be considered as a serious relationship, then there's a problem.

If these friends. then start meddling in your affairs and making decisions in your relationship, it makes it all the more frustrating. As a man you won't know which friend said what and influenced her in this way or that.

All you'll feel is the repercussions.

Different women have different boundaries. Now if a friend of hers wields influential power over your girlfriend and your girlfriend is quite relaxed and easy going, but the friend is uptight and always ready and waiting for drama, the combination can spell disaster for your relationship. If she has multiple friends with similar influence and power, then you might as well say goodbye now.

Women & Their Children

A friend of mine once told me that when your partner has a child, you are no longer number one in your woman's life. You become second best, your child takes your place as number one. When you have another child together, you then become third best and so on and so forth.

Not my words, his.

It is quite natural because as a grown man you should be able to fend for yourself. A newborn baby can't do much other than suck, defecate, cry, and sleep.

They need their parents to survive.

A woman will have just carried this baby in her stomach for approximately 9 months. Other than all the worrying about whether the child will be born healthy and all the other fears of childbirth, she'll be relieved to finally get the child out of her.

Unfortunately, that may not stop a man from feeling neglected.

His woman is now out of bounds for the foreseeable future, sexually, and there's now a baby to look after that will drain all the love, time and energy out of her.

In my opinion, a man should be taking this time to bond with the child and also help lift the burden off of the woman.

Children can bring friction into a once beautiful relationship.

When I was younger two friends of mine had a child and I remember them both arguing over the baby. Both of them complaining that the other spent too much time with the child and that they wouldn't let the other do anything with the child.

They hadn't thought about how to incorporate the child into their relationship. When the baby arrived they followed their natural instincts to dote over the baby, but forgot about understanding each other, working together etc.

A big problem is the dynamics in a relationship change once there's a child in the equation.

We are creatures of habit and you may have gotten used to a certain way of life with your partner. When there's only the two of you to consider, the only issues about going out is finding something to do that you can both appreciate and afford.

Unless a woman has a low libido or the man's rubbish in bed - in which case she may fake having a low libido or the man may make her libido low - sex isn't usually an issue. You can have it anytime, anywhere, if you live alone.

You'll have a routine that works for both of you, this may be no routine at all but as it works for both of you, there's no complaints. Work, family, friends and hobbies are the only real things that may take time away from each other and, other than work, you can usually fit the others around your schedule.

Life is easier and free.

Then, suddenly after months of waiting, a baby rears its head along.

Everything changes.

Both parents, sometimes only the mother, devote their energy, time and attention to the newborn in the house.

Everything now revolves around the baby. If you're lucky enough to have a support system or rich enough to pay for one, then the strains might not be too much to bear. But most mothers want to spend time with their newborns anyway.

A new routine starts to become established,

which focuses on your new baby's wants and needs. If you want to go out on a date you have to have someone to look after the child. Someone you both trust to look after your child suitably.

When you go out as a family, there's now a long checklist to remember so that you don't forget something important for your baby. A man does become second best, but it's something he'll have to get used to. And, if they intend to have more children, then, he'll just have to wait in line.

Or as many men do, he'll cheat. It's easier.

Women who already have a child, or children, are a no-go area for many men. Some brave men will take them on and take them seriously while others will just enjoy the sex.

The problem is many men want to start a family fresh with a woman who doesn't have any yet.

That way it's something special for both of them. It's their first child together. They'll both be learning together and going through a unique experience together, which can bring them closer together, despite what I said above. When two people have to overcome a difficult experience, their bond grows.

They both will implement the way they want to raise their child together. This can also bring its own problems as both parents may have different views on the way a child should be brought up in the world. Several conversations and compromises must be achieved before you decide to have a baby together, in my opinion.

Then, with women that already have children, issues can arise with the new man and the father's child.

The father might feel uncomfortable with another man being around his child and might cause problems for the new guy. He may even use the child, depending on the child's age and the influence he has over them, to turn the child against the new man.

There's also the fact that the new man is not the child's father.

He may feel uncomfortable making decisions for that child. Even if he throws himself in and plays the role of the father he may have issues with the mother if she wants to raise her offspring in a certain way. As mentioned before, this can be an issue with two biological parents, but at least both of them have a 50-50 say on the principles to instil in their children.

The new man doesn't have any rights and may feel marginalised.

A man and a woman might meet and become deeply attracted to each other. They may get on like a house on fire, they may be able to communicate well together. They may enjoy each other's company immensely.

Then, when the man meets the woman's child, for whatever reason the child doesn't take to him. It might not even be the man's fault. That child just might want to see their father with their mother and any other man won't be able to fill his boots. This can sometimes be resolved after some time, with the man being patient and showing the child love throughout.

Even after he does father the child, that child could turn around at any time and say hurtful things like: "You're not my real dad" or "I'm not listening to you, you're not even my father."

That's how grateful children are nowadays.

It's a problem.

Put that together with the difficulties of raising children; the financial costs, as children are expensive, and add in the childcare issues, why would a man willingly put himself in that position, when it's not his child or children, when there's plenty of childless women out there?

Many women might be reading this and ask, if that's the case, why should women go with men that are already fathers?

When it comes to the eyes of the law, when it comes to parenting, the law favours mothers. Unless there's something really wrong in the mother's case, she usually wins custody of the child in a break up.

Many argue this is unfair. I believe it is fair because as I mentioned in an earlier chapter, we are equal, but different. Men with children rarely have custody of their child, which means the scenario is different if a woman meets a man with a child. He may only see his child on the weekends or fortnightly or even less.

A woman is much more likely to have custody of her child if she's broken up with the father.

That's just the way it is.

Getting Ready

I love a woman that takes pride in her appearance. However, there's some beautiful women out there who can't be bothered to make an effort with how they look.

They look unkempt and scruffy.

Their clothes tend not to fit them and they don't suit them either. Their hair's all over the place and their outfits makes Jeremy Corbyn's attire look like James Bond's next outfit in comparison.

These women don't really care to be honest. As far as they're concerned, people should accept them for who they are. The problem about that is people make judgements on how people present themselves. If you look like Worzel Gummidge on a good day most men will not pay you any mind.

Men are aesthetic creatures. We are very visual. If a woman isn't the most attractive person in the world, but if she makes an effort, men are likely to be attracted to her. She may not be stunning, but he'll think she scrubs up well, unless she looks like Lena Hyena, the fake Jessica Rabbit.

A man might not notice that a woman has a

matching handbag to her shoes and that she's coordinated her clothing to pull off a certain look. But he will feel inexplicably attracted to the woman, thinking to himself that she looks classy.

He'll approach her and consider himself lucky if he's got her number. The problem that exists here is that he doesn't realise how long it took for her to get ready.

If these women, attractive and unattractive alike, are going out and have to decide on an outfit, you might not end up going out at all. Or at the very best you'll be extremely late.

Why do women have to try on so many outfits before they can figure out what they are wearing?

If you've bought clothes and tried them on in the shop you should know what they look like. I know these women are trying to look their best, but beauty doesn't take that long.

Getting ready involves having a wash, bath or a shower. Moisturising your skin and applying fragrances. Putting on a bit of face paint. Slipping into an outfit. Doing your hair and that's it. Correct me if I'm wrong.

Now let's add a realistic time-frame to these activities. The wash, bath or shower shouldn't take longer than 30 minutes. Creaming your skin and adding multiple fragrances should take 5 minutes max. A bit of slap on your face, no longer than 15 minutes, 25 minutes if you have to put on nail polish. This is already sounding long in my opinion. Choosing and putting on an outfit shouldn't take longer than 10 minutes, 15 if you've put on weight and need help zipping up. Doing your hair should take another 15 minutes.

Now adding that up it should take between 1 hour and 15 minutes – 1 hour and a half. I'm being very generous with the time here in my opinion because I think it should take an hour to get ready.

Why does it take 2 hours or more for a lot of women to get ready?

It's because they can't make up their mind of what to wear. What should take 30 minutes, can end up taking 1-2 hours, sometimes even longer.

Doing your hair one way, then deciding on another way to then later change it back to the first style is all totally unnecessary. By the way, the order of events may be different for different women, but it'll lead to the same outcome.

Worst of all, is the woman that takes hours to

get ready and still looks a mess. Why bother? You might as well of taken 15 minutes if in the end you look like Boris Johnson on a bad day.

Perhaps it was the way they were raised as a child

Maybe they weren't afforded the opportunity to choose an outfit for themselves.

I am a firm believer in parents parenting their children as they see fit, and being the adult, they generally make better judgements on things than a child would. In fact, it sickens me to see children bullying parents into things they know less about than the parent, but the parent, being a pushover parent, allows the child to take command. I'm not advocating for that.

I'm not an expert in this field, but I believe as a child grows, you should allow them to make some decisions, if you can see their decision makes no sense at all; like they want to go out wearing their bikini when it's -5c outside and snowing, you educate them and tell them why it's not a good idea, then help them choose something more suitable.

As they get older they should be able to put a sensible outfit together without taking all year to get ready.

Shop Shop Shop

In my experience I've noticed that women like shopping.

In fact, they don't just like it - they love it. It's like a hobby, in place of watching a match or playing football in the park with some mates, which a man might do. Women love to shop.

It can be a very expensive hobby.

Some women plan shopping.

First by looking online, this may involve buying a few bits and pieces while they're online. Once they've examined the whole catalogue of different collections online, they'll visit the stores to try things on.

By the way, this expensive shopping hobby can be done alone or with one or more friends. It's an activity to them. Like an adventure. It can actually vastly brighten up their day. The equivalent for a man might be to chat up a woman and have sex with her on the same day.

You can see the difference in a woman after she's had a good shop. Her eyes glow, she'll hardly be able to contain her delight. A smile will fix itself to her face. She'll be in a good mood and if it's not that time of the month, her man might be in for a treat that night.

Sounds great.

Not if you're the one paying for it.

Or even if she's paying for it, but you know she can't really afford it, which might mean that you'll have to indirectly pay for it by subsidising her until payday. If, as a man, you're a saver and she's a spender, then she'll piss you off all of the time.

Women can spend a lot of money in a short space of time.

But guess what? She'll buy clothes that she'll only wear once, or worse than that, she'll buy things she'll never wear. That's right. Women can be terribly wasteful, just so they can enjoy the buzz of buying something new.

While a man might be saving for a deposit on a house, she'll be saving for a handbag and matching shoes. Believe it or not, that could end up being a big chunk of the house deposit money.

If a woman knows that a man will scrutinise her purchases and possibly complain, she'll just buy them sneakily. She'll pay in cash and hide them in her handbag, instead of using a card and accepting the shops brand carrier-bag. Or she'll leave it somewhere safe at work, then when it's her birthday or something she'll say it's a gift from someone.

Women are not just pretty faces. They're sneaky little devils.

Another problem about a woman shopping is if she drags her man along. He'll be thinking of plenty of other things he could be doing with his time while she'll be marching around shopping, tugging him along without a care in the world.

A man will be bored stiff.

He'll be wondering why she has to go into every shop, try almost everything on, in all the shops, ask for his opinion a million times and then go back to the first shop they visited to buy something. Or she'll buy something from one shop, then walk around trying to find matching items. If she can't find any matching items, she'll bring back the item she bought for a refund.

For a man, this is like watching paint dry.

He'll be wondering if any of these shops sell guns, so he can buy one to shoot himself in the head, to put himself out of his misery.

To other women this is like having an orgy. They'll all try stuff on, comment on what they think looks good or bad, ask each other's opinions, ask the sales assistance opinion and even ask other shoppers their opinion. It's like a field trip to them.

If you're a man and you can't remember your Mum doing something similar when you were younger, take my advice: Never go shopping with a woman.

They'll ask you trick questions like: "What do you think?". If she likes it, but you say you don't, she'll be upset with you, if she doesn't like it and you do, she'll tell you why you shouldn't like it.

You can't win either way.

Trust me, it's best you don't go in the first place.

Miss Independent

I once went to a debate where people were discussing the roles of men and women in relationships. A woman held the stage to say how successful she was and how independent she was. She said she didn't need a man to buy her anything, as she could afford to buy things for herself, and she didn't need a man to do anything as she could do things for herself.

She did mention, however, that she was single and looking for the right guy.

The next person to take the stage was a man who aimed his message to the woman and asked her: "What do you want a man for?" He said that men wanted to be desired and relied upon. They wanted to be useful and appreciated for their input into the relationship. "If you can do it all yourself, why do you want a man?"

I have to agree with this man. If you have it all and don't need me for any reason, then what am I doing in your life other than providing sexual services? If you're that successful you can easily pay an escort for that.

Then, there is no need to be in a traditional

relationship. We can be friends with benefits.

Now I'm not saying women shouldn't strive to achieve or improve themselves. I'm all for people developing themselves and enhancing their prospects in life. What a lot of women fail to realise is that vulnerability is an attractive quality. Men like to be a hero, a woman with vulnerability gives us that feeling of being the protector, the provider.

It makes us feel useful.

If I'm of no use to a woman, then I'd rather be with someone who I can be of use to.

I like a woman that cries on my shoulder every now and again, not literally and not too often if it is literally, I may add. I like to go through a journey with a woman where I help her improve and progress as a person and vice versa, then we see the growth in the both of us. I like growing together, it can bring you closer together as a couple.

I like when a woman asks my advice, only every now and again, not every time they have a decision to make. Although I can't stand when a woman asks for my advice, and I probe her into understanding the situation clearly in order to give her the best advice. I then offer my advice, only for her to ignore my advice and do the complete opposite.

If you're not going to take heed of my advice, don't ask for it!

Some women are just too independent for their own good. Sometimes that brings an aura around them that is slightly unappealing. They act like they know it all and nobody can tell them anything. There can be a coldness to these women and they might not even realise it.

As a man I like a woman that's warm and approachable. That way I can get close to her and feel comfortable around her. I like a woman that feels a little bit vulnerable, then I'm able to comfort her. I like a woman that seeks my knowledge, then I'm able to advise her. A woman that's a tiny bit insecure, then I'm able to compliment her and help boost her esteem.

She feels loved and I feel wanted and needed and we both feel closer to each other.

Perfect.

You Bitch

Not you men, just you women.

Don't go getting yourself worked up having a heart attack, it's a joke.

Seriously though, why are women, in general, so bitchy?

Is it something in their genetic make-up, social conditioning, or their upbringing? I see no need for it. Does bitchiness stem from some form of insecurity? Maybe these women don't feel good about themselves so they feel the need to belittle others or hurt them out of spite.

I'm not saying guys can't be bitchy because they can, and I have to say, especially gay men. I have nothing against gay men, but in my experience they can be bitchier than women. Overall, it seems to be a familiar trait with many females.

Some women will even tell you that they're bitchy!

A number of women are just bitchy regardless of who they are dealing with. They are just naturally bitchy. They don't care who you are, they are just bitches. It's as if they can't help it, or worse, they don't see the need to. They act as if being a spiteful, mean person is something worth bragging about.

They'll smile in your face, then talk negatively about you behind your back. A lot of them won't say anything to your face, but they'll spend an endless amount of time criticising you as soon as you're out of earshot.

If you get wind of what they are saying and confront them, many of them will deny it unless you have overwhelming evidence; such as a recording of a phone call with them mouthing off, otherwise they'll swear on their life that they've never said a bad thing about you.

Me, personally, if I can say something behind your back, I might as well say it to your face. If I've got something to say, I'll say it. Why pretend to be nice, and a lot of the time overly so, when you can't stand someone's guts.

I don't hate anybody, but some people do tend to get on my nerves from time to time, so I will politely tell them to refrain from doing whatever it is they do that annoys me and then we can get along fine after the issue has been resolved.

Women will pretend to adore someone, boosting up this person's confidence in their friendship, only to bad-mouth them 5 minutes later. Essentially, these women are playing with the emotions of those involved, giving them a false sense of security. This only intensifies the sense of betrayal they'll feel when they find out the woman never liked them in the first place, but led them on, pulling on their heart-strings.

Some women are only bitchy to women.

Lucky enough for us men they treat us like kings and their female counterparts are treated with the same scrutiny the ugly step-sisters gave Cinderella. Although they lead the victim of their artificial behaviour down a path of confusion, due to their two-face antics.

Why these women are only bitchy to their own sex is beyond me.

A lot of these women tend to have male friends and not many female friends, if any at all. Maybe because they've totally destroyed their friendships with other women and can only build friendships with men as they can't help but spoil their friendships with those of their gender.

It's sad really when you think about it.

The spiteful behaviour of some women is unacceptable. I've read about guys having their private parts chopped off because of infidelity. I understand that being cheated on isn't to be taken lightly. It's heart breaking, embarrassing and demoralising. But chopping off a man's private part isn't the answer.

Infidelity isn't the only thing that brings spite out of these women.

Absence enrages them also. It may only have been a day or two of no contact, and you may have explained the situation beforehand; but depending on the emotional state of the woman, that time period is long enough. You could go to her house to find all your clothes cut up because that's what she decided to do to entertain herself whilst you were away.

To be honest, any number of things could spark these bitchy, spiteful breed of women into action.

If you make the mistake of saying something in the wrong tone or they misinterpret a message you sent them, that's enough for them to go on a malicious spree to get at you. Any number of things could be the consequence, from keying your car to your gadgets being thrown about and getting stamped on.

I'm fearful of leaving my belongings at a woman's place or living with a woman because you never know what these women are capable of or what might set them off.

As I said earlier, I love women I just can't live with them and I can't live without them.

I Am Saying She's A Gold Digger

Yeah, that's right, there's many women out there who won't even sniff at you if your money isn't strong and long.

As far as I know, so far, men cannot bear children. And, I say this, because technology moves so quickly and humans are experimenting with so many strange things that it seems like nothing is impossible. If you're reading this in the future and men can now bear children, my bad.

The reason I mention this is that a lot of women that want to have children, look at a man and wonder if he will be able to provide while she's on maternity leave, and possibly longer, as some women struggle with the thought of working while they could be looking after their child.

Many would prefer to be able to afford to look after their child and take a break from work, which I think is understandable. It doesn't always work out that way, but it's a completely reasonable goal to strive towards.

A woman doesn't want to end up with a man who isn't making a decent living, or worse, not even trying. Yes, there are many bums out there that are not too interested in finding work, although at the time of writing, David Cameron, George Osbourne and co are making it rather difficult not to go out and earn your daily bread; in the UK that is, I'm not sure about elsewhere.

This chapter is not about a woman that's looking for a man that's working or working towards accomplishing a thing or two in his life. This chapter is about the piranhas that will empty your bank account and leave you penniless in as quick a time that is humanly possible.

They'll see a poorly dressed ugly guy and not pay him any mind until they see him take out the pinkies or jump into his rich man mobile. Then, all of a sudden, out of the blue, they're interested. Their eyes brighten up, their bodies uplift from the dead stiffness that it was just encumbering and their personalities take on a warm bubbly charm that was previously totally nonchalant and antisocial.

In effect they smell blood. Only this blood is the colour of money and has the queen's face on it.

Now to be fair many women like successful men. I wouldn't cast them all in the category of Gold Diggers. There's something about successful men that's attractive to women.

Confidence.

Women like confident men.

Men that are achieving or have achieved have an air about them which attracts women. If, as a man, you walk down the road when not much is going on in your life and you're single, many women won't look in your direction.

If, on the other hand, you're walking down the road with a stunningly beautiful woman and you're feeling secure and successful in your career, then all of a sudden women tend to cast their eyes on you. Even if you're walking down the road alone, you let off an ambience, one that makes you more attractive and draws other women's attention to you. It doesn't necessarily mean that women will know you're in a relationship, but you'll still be more attractive than if you're feeling down.

It's like if you're in a job you're more employable than if you're unemployed. People want people that other people want. If no-one wants you, you're not an attractive proposition. You're unwanted. Maybe someone that feels sorry for you might pity you and show you some attention because no-one else will. But on the whole you're not that much of an asset.

It's not nice, but that's life.

This chapter is excluding that certain confidence that women are attracted to.

These blood thirsty vultures are not that kind of women. They couldn't care less whether you are confident or not. Not all men with a few bob are confident. All these women care about is whether they can get a healthy lump sum when you die and the rest while you're alive.

In fact, some of them would prefer if you're not confident. You then become easy prey.

The little bit of attention they pretend to give you, will make you feel wanted and loved and without too much work for these manipulating evil witches. They'll be able to make or break you as they are the ones that make you feel worthwhile. If you don't give them what they want, they play all sorts of mind games including heart wrenching guilt trips and emotional blackmail.

If you have family and friends, some of them will smell her cunningness from a mile off. But unfortunately a lot of men's brains are located in their penises. Family and friends are not offering great head and the best sex that they've had in a lifetime. This money grabbing predator knows that and will secure your allegiances with heavy compensation.

Some of them are even smarter than the ones just mentioned. Maybe they've had more experience or maybe they just thought it out better.

They'll actually charm the socks off of your friends and family. Everyone will be none the wiser. But the woman will be more the richer. No-one will speak badly of her because she's already wrapped them around her manipulating fingers, counting the money as you read.

Some of these women have done this many times before. They've been married and divorced a few times to wealthy men. The pay-out(s) may have been pretty healthy, but it's in these women's blood. We are creatures of habit. We do what we know and these women know how to bleed men dry. It's what they do. They enjoy it.

They're serial gold diggers.

Unfortunately, your loved ones will be heartbroken watching you ruin your life and give away fortunes just for a pretty face and a little bit of pussy. It sounds crude, but it's the truth.

Is it a price worth paying?

You do have some women on the other hand who aren't just after a man's money. They may actually like him and they're not as ruthless as the women mentioned above. That doesn't stop them from relying on men financially.

They never offer to pay, in fact, they expect a man to pay for everything. Whether they're on a date or they're in a relationship they expect the man to pay all the time regardless of his financial position in life. If the man refuses to pay for something they call him tight or stingy.

Some men have a plan.

They realise that if they save up and invest they will be able to spend the profit of the investment without losing money. It may take a while to get there, but if they're smart with their money they can have a nice future, which will include whoever their partner is at the time.

These women can't see that far into the future. They want it all and they want it all now.

They want Louboutin shoes, Michael Kors bags, Tiffany jewellery and all the other luxury items that women crave for. They don't mind watching their partner struggle to pay for these things even though it's seriously hurting his pocket.

This type of woman tends to reward a man that furnishes her with presents; with sex and affection. A lot of the time it's not even a calculated act. It's her natural reaction to receiving gifts. If you spend money on her, she'll be nice to you.

She has a mind-set that feasts today and lives in famine tomorrow.

Even though, if they chose the reversal of this, they'd have more chance of extravagance in abundance in the future. But as far as they're concerned their nails need doing now. They want it all now without a thought of tomorrow.

They'll end up leaving the guy, not directly over money. Not because they no longer like him, but because of arguments over money that cause friction in the relationship.

He wants to save to be able to invest in their future like Chris Gardner in The Pursuit of Happiness. She wants to spend like Rebecca Bloomfield in Confessions of a Shopaholic.

Mood Swings

When two people first meet and are attracted to each other, they usually put their best foot forward. They're on their best behaviour trying to charm the socks off each other. They mention all the good things about themselves and usually neglect to mention any bad things.

It's perfectly normal that the everyday version of themselves differs slightly from what they portray in the beginning. And, as time goes by, their true colours start to reveal themselves. This doesn't necessarily mean that they are awful in comparison, it just shows they're human and have faults, like everyone else.

When you get involved in a relationship you need to be aware that you're literally entering a relationship with more than one woman. I'm not talking about her female family and friends. I'm referring to the one woman. Although she is one person in the physical form, she'll have a plethora of moods that will change her personality at the flick of a switch.

In fact, they'll be so many versions of her you will wonder who you're coming home to.

A woman may start off portraying the shy and timid side of herself. She'll naturally be like that until she starts to feel comfortable. Then, she'll open up and show another side of herself, possibly the cheeky side. This is still relatively normal since she will show different sides of her main mood as she begins to trust you and open up.

Women's moods change all the time and these mood changes, bring a transformation. A woman may appear quiet and serene most of the time, only for an event to trigger something inside her to change her mood. The next minute she'll be screaming and shouting and you'll be wondering why.

She'll usually have her main mood. The one you will get to know and recognise. Hopefully that's the version of her you like, otherwise I'd start looking for a new woman.

I'm not saying men don't get moody, but there's a limit to their moods. Women actually transform into a totally different person and they can transform into many different characters.

If you piss a woman off, and try to talk to her, she'll switch on you like Regan in the Exorcist.

She won't even notice the change a lot of the

time, but because you're at the end of it, you will.

She'll be talking about something, then she'll touch on a touchy subject, her voice will quiver and she'll be crying like a newborn. All out of the blue.

What's that all about?

From the normal person you were dealing with, you now have to deal with a big cry baby, who needs comforting and consoling.

They'll flick from one character to the next because her mood is constantly changing. Luckily for men if you say something that puts her in a good mood you can change her mood from something negative to something positive.

This works sometimes, not all of the time.

Throughout your relationship you'll most probably get to meet the prudent version, who believes sex is dirty. But she'll also have a nymphomaniac version of herself, which the right guy can bring out of her.

I once had a female boss who was as nice as pie with me.

A colleague warned me that she could be a real bitch when she wanted to be. I'd never come across this side of her I didn't think anything of it. Then, one day she literally changed from my nice boss into the raging Hulk. I'm not even sure what made her change as I didn't do anything wrong.

While she was the Hulk, I was shit scared of her. Every morning I didn't want to go into work. Then, one day I thought to myself, I'm a grown man, why should I fear my boss? She was like the Hulk, with me, for a couple of months and then, just like that, she changed back into Bruce Banner.

The funniest thing is, in the time she was the Hulk with me, she was Bruce Banner with everyone else. Then, she was Bruce Banner with me and the Hulk with someone else.

Weird.

I was lucky because there were only two sides of her. Good cop and bad cop. In relationships I've found women have multiple moods and each one needs to be handled accordingly in order for a man to live tranquilly.

Let's be fair, a lot of women's emotions are all over the place. They're ultra-sensitive; all sorts of situations leave them in tears. If they're not in tears, they're mouthing off, shouting and screaming like some football hooligan.

Women study men's voices like a computer becoming artificially intelligent. All it takes is for a slight change in the tone of a man's voice and they're assuming things in their mind and taking offence when there was none intended.

They might feel neglected because you haven't paid them enough attention, in their minds. Which in reality means that you left her side, on a night out, for 5 minutes. All of a sudden, she'll accuse you of not caring about her anymore.

Women might be more mature than men, but they take everything personally.

Everything.

That Time Of The Month

That dreaded time of the month.

Men and women hate it.

Women hate it because of the emotional effect it has on them, not to mention the physical strain it puts on them. No-one likes to bleed, worse is having to bleed from your genitals once a month, sometimes more, for those women with irregular cycles.

Men hate it because it equals no sex.

If a man is not living with a woman, but they're having some form of sexual relationship and she invites him to stay over, in his mind sex must be on the agenda; except if she's invited him over previously and it wasn't on the agenda.

Even so, a man will still be hopeful and believe "it's on tonight".

When he gets there and everything seems quite normal he still thinks positively about putting some motion in her ocean. That is until they start getting ready for bed and he notices she's wearing some oversized granny knickers.

At that moment in time he literally wants to

put his clothes back on and walk back out through the door, unless she wears granny knickers all the time, in that case he'll be sick of the sight of them. Then, again if for some weird reason he's got a fetish for them, then he won't be bothered.

Most men will think she's on the wind up.

Why invite a red blooded male to stay over, only for you to be on your period. It's different if the man has been forewarned. Otherwise, it feels like a woman is just taking the piss.

If a man hasn't had sexual relations with a woman he may not mind as much, as he'll see it as a step in the right direction. If she's inviting him into her bed for the first time, he'll most probably consider it healthy progress, although he may still be disappointed.

Another reason men dislike that wonderful time of the month, is the transformation that takes place within a woman. Whatever a woman may be like normally, when they're on their period most of them transform into some form of monster.

I understand that this is an annoying time for a woman and that her hormones are all over the place. But as far as I can see, women tend to blame all their erratic behaviour and their aggressive outbursts at these times, on their period.

They use that line like someone that cheats might use alcohol and expect everyone to forgive and forget. "It was that time of the month, I know you don't get a period, but surely you can understand". That's the type of thing a woman may say after their hostile screaming and shouting sessions.

Women can be extremely nasty around that time of the month, I don't mean nasty as in dirty or unclean, I mean nasty as in malicious. So much so that it feels like they think they have a licence to do and say as they please without fear of judgement or repercussions.

They'll say stuff that will put the whole relationship in jeopardy, such as they slept with someone else or your child isn't yours and when their periods over they'll be like: "Did I actually say that? You know it's not true honey, it was just that my hormones were all over the place" etc., etc.

That's if a man sticks around long enough for her period to be over and hear her unimaginative explanation.

The most reserved of women will transform and deteriorate into someone resembling a mouthy guest on the Jeremy Kyle show. Let's make no mistake, women can be absolutely vile.

At the same time a lot of women want their man around them while they're going through this painful experience. Maybe because they want to take it out on him. Who knows, but I can tell you he'd rather be on the other side of the earth.

Sex

Sex is the most pertinent factor of a relationship for the vast majority of men. The problem is, while it may be an ingredient for women, it's not unusual for it to be less significant in a companionship compared to men.

For men, sex can rank up to 90% of importance in a relationship and the other 10% will make up of all the other aspects; sometimes sex is even higher on the list than that.

Not all men, but I would say a large percentage of men regard sex as extremely high on the agenda in a partnership.

I mean, it's pretty clear. I am a man and the biggest chapter in this book is dedicated to the subject.

It doesn't mean men only want women for sex, it means it's a seriously important feature in a relationship. Just like having a man treating them respectfully may be high on the priority list for women.

The problem here is that, to a lot of women, sex isn't that important.

They want good sex when it happens, but they can live without it. Don't get me wrong - there are women out there with high sex drives, and good sex is high on some women's agenda in a relationship, but for the majority of them, there are plenty other areas that are just as important, if not more.

For a man, this is seriously frustrating. Being intimate with our partner often makes us feel loved, wanted and appreciated. Usually when a man is getting good sex often, from his partner, things feel like they are running smoothly. He feels happy and confident.

For women, this is just not the case. In fact, it's almost the exact opposite.

When things are running smoothly in other areas of the relationship, when they feel loved, wanted and appreciated, then they feel it's ok to open their legs and welcome a man in. But, many men don't have a clue about the variables that influence a woman's decision to lie down with them.

I can hear some men thinking: "what other areas?"

Can everyone see how this is a big problem?

Sex means totally different things to both sexes.

Sex is the icing on the cake for women, but sex is the cake for men. Women have to be in the mood while a man is in that mood most of the time and even if he's not, it doesn't take much to change his mind. A little subtle persuasion.

Now, as a man, I hate lying down in bed with a partner, and in my mind, I'm thinking can I or can't I? This will be because either she's rejected me sexually previously, or she's a new partner that I'm unsure of. Not to mention that she could be on her period - I can't keep up with those monthly cycles which can be unreliable anyway.

If it's because of rejection this is totally frustrating because, and I truly believe I'm speaking for the majority of men out there, what's the point of having a partner only to be unsure of whether you can have sex with her? It makes bedtimes feel awkward, and you might as well still be on a first date.

Better still, a one night stand. At least then, you'd still be getting intimate.

A man wants a woman to allow him to do what he wants, sexually, when he wants.

If that happens to be every night and every morning, when a woman isn't on her period, then that just happens to be the case. A lot of men only last a couple of minutes anyway. If you get it twice a day, that's about 4-5 minutes a day excluding foreplay and afterplay, if he even does that, as those are just extras and not the main activity.

Obviously there are a few studs out there that last a little bit or a lot longer and some guys are generous with fore and afterplay. In that case he's most probably a considerate lover and you should be lapping it up.

A man might not even want sex every day and every night, but when he wants it, it's almost as if he needs it.

The other day I was discussing with some mates, why women who are not on their period turn around and tell a man we're not having sex, but I'll give you head.

What's that all about?

Let me get this right, sexual intercourse involves both of us getting physical pleasure. You giving me head involves only me getting pleasure. Why would you opt out of getting pleasure to only give pleasure? None of us could figure that out.

I'm baffled.

You never hear a man say he'll give you oral

and you don't have to do anything. If he does say that, it's a trick, to get you all worked up and excited so he can slip inside you, and you'll be too horny to decline.

Another thing that is opposite for women with sex is its effect. After sex, a man just wants to roll over and fall asleep. I'm sure this is due to some chemical reaction that occurs after a man ejaculates. For women, on the other hand, it makes them wide awake. If a man's lucky the most she'll require is a kiss and a cuddle.

She may want more sex, not necessarily intercourse, but she might want more attention; a massage or something else that she likes. This is the last thing on most guys mind because they're no longer thinking, they're half way to dreamland. Women want to talk at this stage while we men want to start snoring.

For women, sex is the 'wake-up' call they were waiting for. They're ready to get up and go for a jog, walk to work, start cooking or just have a good old chat.

If you're lucky enough to get a guy who's willing to talk to you and massage you after sex, marry him. Tend to his every need and want.

This man is gold dust.

In my experience women tend to prefer a seeing to in the morning, unless there are children that will burst into the room or that sleep there - those women tend to not want sex at all. At night-time they find it keeps them awake, which can have the reverse effect of them wanting to keep you awake, when you're at your most irritable.

That is, unless you thoroughly work them out until they're exhausted.

Once you ejaculate don't give them a break, go again, straight away, don't wait for it to go soft, keep that momentum going. Make sure you do the things she likes that get her to squirt or orgasm or both. Play with her clit or finger her g-spot, whatever tickles her fancy. You'll most probably triple the time you just lasted, and then she'll be too tired to keep you awake talking.

That's just a little advice to the fellowman out there.

As mentioned above, periods are another problem with women. No, I'm not even talking directly about the period itself, there's already a chapter about that. I'm sure women hate them as much as men, in fact, it's clear they hate them a lot more than men, but I'm talking about the fact that a woman may not be in the mood for sex all month, until around the time she starts to bleed.

What is that all about?

I'm sure it's not their fault, it must be part of their genetic makeup. The problem is, when a woman is on her period most guys want to run a mile and come and see them when the volcano has stopped erupting.

This sounds cruel, but it's the truth.

A man most probably won't admit it and he'll stick around you and might grin and bear it for the duration, if that's what's required, but it's the last place he wants to be.

You're moody and out of bounds, yet you're horny and wouldn't mind him rumbling in your jungle. Not most men's cup of tea, although I'm sure there are guys out there with weird fetishes that wouldn't mind that.

Men in general are aesthetic, especially when it comes to sex. They want sex in the daytime with the curtains or blinds open or with the light on at night. Women in general, are insecure about a part or parts of their body or face that the guy most probably isn't bothered about, and as a result of this, want to make love in the pitch black.

Total darkness.

What's the point in that?

Why would a man chat up a woman he fancies physically only to not see the same beautiful face and body whilst getting his groove on? Can you women see how that is counterproductive?

We want to see that beautiful face of yours and your facial expressions while we're penetrating you. We love to see that look of lust or love in your eyes and your boobs bouncing up and down or your bum jiggling.

It turns us on.

It brings the animal out in us. We love it.

Unless a man needs a magnifying glass and tweezers to insert his penis into you, most guys love to see what's going on.

That brings me to another point. Women that don't make an effort in the bedroom.

I'm not even talking about sexually. I'm talking visually. Some of these pyjamas that women wear to bed are totally off-putting. Men are very visual creatures by nature. We like to see a woman dressed up in stockings and suspenders. All that lace and sexy underwear, it doesn't matter if you're not gonna be wearing it by the time we've finished, it's alluring.

Yet if you see how some women dress for bed with their partners you'd believe they were celibate.

Some wear what I can only describe as turbans to bed to keep their hair in order. Fair enough, they might be trying to save time in the morning; so they take less time getting ready, but wear your hair out once in a while. Get your hair done nice and pretty and wear it to bed. If you've never done this most men will appreciate this enormously.

Others go to bed looking like Cinderella before she went to the ball. They wear home clothes to bed. Some of these clothes look like rags refused by charity shops. Very attractive.

That's sarcasm by the way.

If you can't be bothered or can't afford to buy a pretty bedtime outfit, don't wear anything at all.

Men love naked women. It's a fact.

As I mentioned earlier, men want open access to do whatever they please. Now some men's fetishes in my opinion are ludicrous. With the advent of porn a lot of men's boundaries are going out the window. A lot of women feel uncomfortable doing certain things, and if a guy wants to piss on you or do something worse, so you should be.

But I'm sure sex is on the mind. Whatever you think about, sex has an effect on your boundaries and what you are willing to try. I'll get into trying things in a moment, but some women think sex is dirty. I cannot agree with this mind-set, although they're perfectly entitled to this opinion - as I am mine.

How did they think they were born? Do they believe that a stalk flew by and dropped them off at the doorstep? I'm very sorry to burst their bubble, but their parents got busy in the bedroom and so did their grandparents and so on and so forth.

Sex is enjoyable so that animals, including humans, are enticed to reproduce. It's a loving act between two people, sometimes more nowadays, to be intimate and feel close to one another.

Some women have too many issues surrounding sex.

They might believe it's dirty and only want to indulge in it when it's time to reproduce. Or they think about so many other stuff during sex that they don't enjoy the act itself.

They're lying there wondering if they're making too much noise. That's fair enough if the whole family is next door, sitting in silence waiting for your appearance. But if the house is empty with no one soon to return, what's the problem?

The number of things that can niggle in a woman's mind before, during and after sex is too much to mention. A woman may even enjoy sex in the build-up and during the act, only for a man to face repercussions for it afterwards, and sometimes that's not even the same day that may be days later, after she over thinks thoughts in her mind.

The next time you attempt to sleep with her, she'll reject you because she didn't like the way she felt after the last session. Not because of how she felt before or during, but after.

Having sex with some women can come with a minefield of issues when really all you want, is to be intimate and have an easy life. Don't women want an easy life too? I'm sure they do, everybody does. Then, why complicate sex? Just enjoy it and feel closer to your partner.

But, getting back to boundaries, it's not

uncommon that men want a woman that will let them do anything they want. Not a woman that complains about doing it in this or that position. Women can really suck the fun out of sex while we men want them to suck the hell out of us.

She doesn't do this and she doesn't do that. Don't let little things prohibit you from having fun. It's all in the mind. Explore each other's bodies and see what you both like and what you dislike. Most women like men to take control in the bedroom (unless of course she's a dominatrix) and most men like to take control. Allow him to, you never know, you might just enjoy it.

I'm not one for having a sexually aggressive partner. I say this because sometimes women want sex, but if they're too aggressive or direct in their approach it can be off-putting for me. Now don't get me wrong; I have awoken to a woman with my manhood in her mouth and I can tell you that I loved it.

That's the way to wake up.

I don't mind a woman making the first move, but it's all about how she does it. If I come home to find her in sexy lingerie and a seductive look in her eyes, I'm hardly going to say no. If on the other hand, she's dressed in rags like the Flintstones and she asks me "Are you gonna do it or not?" this is less likely to arouse me.

I suppose this is a subjective area, but I personally prefer the less brutal approach. In fact, I love to take the lead. And, so do many other men.

If you're a woman and you're unhappy with your man's performance in bed, don't demand better sex. Gently assist him. Tell him seductively what you like and what you want him to do to you. Guide his hands across your body in the places you want them to go.

Unless a couple are planning on having as many children as the Waltons or they only have sex when it's time to reproduce then most couples need to use some form of contraception.

If you don't really know each other or you're not in a serious committed relationship, then a condom is most probably the best choice to use.

And, if we were to give totally equal opportunities, then a woman might wear a femidom. I've said this before, but although we're equal, we are different. It might be equal to expect a woman to use a femidom as many women expect a man to use a condom, but we're different. Technically, a femidom is the equivalent to a condom, but how many people have used one?

Now that is out of the way, back to the point I was making. If you're in a long-term serious relationship, then the problem with some women is they still expect a condom to be the contraception of choice.

How rubbish is that?

If I wanted to make love to a rubber balloon, I would. But I don't. I want to make love to my partner. There are many different contraceptive choices out there for women. But some of them refuse to take any for whatever reasons and leave their man having sex that could be a lot more enjoyable.

Some women won't even try anything at all.

They just point blank refuse.

Speaking as a man, sex with a condom and sex without a condom are two different experiences. One is ok and the other one is out of this world.

I know which one I prefer.

Suffocating Women

No I'm not endorsing violence against women, as the title of this chapter might suggest, however annoying they may be. But what is with some women? They're so clingy, it's uncomfortable. They're like those toddlers that won't let their mothers go to the toilet alone without having a tantrum resembling an epileptic fit.

A man can't go anywhere without these women wanting to come. As much as it's nice to be adored and wanted this goes beyond that and feels unhealthy.

If you try to get out of bed they ask you where you're going. If you're in the house with them, but you choose to be in a different room, it's like you've broken some unwritten law. They start questioning you about why you don't want to be with them.

Either that or they follow you.

If you have one of these women in your life, you'll struggle to get stuff done.

You'll be doing something that needs your undivided attention, like work on a laptop, and these women won't leave you alone. Being a bloke that can't multitask, this guarantees that I won't get anything done. And, if you try and shoo them away nicely, politely or even lovingly, no matter how you tell them, they'll be offended.

They'll try and make you feel guilty.

I'm actually an affectionate person, but I'm not one to have a woman suffocating me with their affections all the time. Don't get me wrong, I like cuddling and kissing and spending time with a significant woman in my life, but I don't want to be stuck to her all day everyday like a Siamese twin.

Have you ever had one of those moments where you're struggling to get rid of cling film sticking to you and as you seem to take it off, it attaches itself back onto you from a different angle? These women are just like that.

Extremely hard to get rid of.

If you manage to get away from them for any length of time, they'll be messaging you 5 minutes later - if not calling. If you fail to message them back within 5 seconds they're complaining about neglect.

They'll call you and you'll have a long meaningful conversation. The call will eventually end and you'll go to the toilet or something. Little do you know, they're already on the phone, calling you again.

What is wrong with these women? We just spoke 1 minute ago, what big event happened within that time that merits a call-back. Fair enough if they forget to say something in the hour and a half conversation before, but when this is a regular occurrence it's just plain annoying.

Why do some women insist on having marathon phone calls?

When you're speaking to these women and you want to end the conversation, there's all sorts of emotional blackmail they start to throw at you. If you stay on the phone, you end up surrendering the things you need to do just for a little bit of peace and quiet. If you end the conversation, which may only be possible if you put down the phone without saying a proper goodbye, as the women involved refuses to do so, then you're likely to feel bad because of the guilt trip these women put on you.

If a man doesn't feel that he's spent a minimum of half hour to 1 hour of time speaking to you, he might actually call you a bit more often.

When these women are not messaging or

calling you, they're doing their next favourite obsession when they're not in your presence, stalking you online.

They'll search your social media accounts to see if you've updated your status or waiting to see if the 'd' has turned into a 'r' on the message they sent you 1 second ago. If you haven't updated your status, they're stalking your page to see who else liked your status or picture or who's following you.

They're like the social media Police.

Sometimes these women will start abusing other women that are following you, or who like your status or send you a complimentary comment on a picture or something.

They'll start sending death threats to some female cousin you forgot to tell them about. Or the threats might be a little more subtle; "LEAVE MY MAN ALONE OR ELSE!" Next minute your cousin will be asking you what's up with your crazy girlfriend?

And, God forbid the 'd' changes into a 'r' in a message and you don't text back straight away. Expect a right old bollicking.

They don't seem to realise the realities of modern day life. You might not have time to write back a comprehensive answer as you're busy, so you read it and get on with what you are doing with the mental note to reply later. If you get away with not replying straight away, God save you if you forget completely with the busy day you've been having. They'll be on you like a hyena on a rotten half-eaten zebra carcass.

Some of these totally insecure women will be searching through your clothes pockets looking for clues of infidelity. They'll watch you type in your pins and passwords and memorise them. Then, they'll comb through all your interactions with the world trying to find a discrepancy of some sort.

If they find nothing at all, some of them will still find something to be upset about, like why do you put an 'x' at the end of your messages to females. Why are you hacking into my accounts like Edward Snowden in the first place?

Others will keep quiet and wait for firm evidence, which they may never find as there is nothing to find, and start building a case against you like the Crown Prosecution Service. With all the things that you're busy doing, you'll wonder where they find the time to be so proactive in their detective work. They'll be tracking your smart phones location history trying to find out where you spend your time away from them.

Obviously, these women need some sort of therapy. Anyone who continuously calls your phone back to back and leaves you with 20+ missed calls, and there's no emergency to attend to, has serious psychological issues in my opinion.

Guys, as much as you might like the attention to begin with, in the long run these women will haunt your life. Take my advice, if she seems too clingy, then you should cut it off as soon as possible; otherwise she'll end up being everywhere you go before you're even there, just like Pepé le Pew, the skunk that followed the cat around in those old school cartoons.

Glutton For Punishment

You get these women who say they want a nice guy, but obviously that's not what they want. They are attracted to guys who treat them like dirt, they love it and they hate it at the same time.

Bittersweet.

Yet they will keep on going back until they're so resentful, aggrieved, hurt, vex and bitter that they end up doing spiteful things, like keying up his car or burning his clothes. It clearly would have been better if they just left before things started to turn them into twisted, sour, spiteful bitches.

This particular set of women seem to love getting hurt. They say they don't, but surely they must do. They only go for guys that will hurt them in one way or another. In fact, they're like a magnet that attracts cunts, and not the genital type, which would probably be better for all involved; but the male type.

These are the women that put the meat into the phrase: Nice guys never get the girl. Why? Because these women are just not interested in nice guys. All they want is a 'Bad Boy' who will walk all over them and break their heart.

They love it.

Their friends and family will continuously try to set them up with nice guys, but there's always something wrong with them. Like maybe they turn up too early or he's too nice. They say stuff like: "He kept on saying sorry" or "He's too nice, I don't think he'd be able to handle me". How can you be too nice? The truth of the matter is, these men would most probably treat them like a Queen and be there for them in their times of need.

These women don't want that. They want a guy who's emotionally unavailable, who's gonna turn up late, not pay too much interest in them and who most probably has a few other women on the go already. That's why he knows just what to say and how to act, to get these women tripping over themselves to be with him.

The nice guys are pushed to the side or get stuck in the friend zone.

They'll be putting in months of hard work and effort to try to start a serious, committed, long term relationship with one of these women; only for the woman to reject all of his honest advances and look elsewhere. They let him hang along and stick him in the friend zone.

Meanwhile a Bad Boy will stroll up and have her dropping her knickers at a moment's notice and giving him her heart, her mind and her body with all her love included. A lot of these Bad Boys don't even make much effort. I suppose they don't need to. If that's what these women wanted they would have gone for the nice guy ages ago. Instead, they allow themselves to be swept up in a guy that will never truly love them. Then, they'll complain that they never get a nice guy.

Treat them mean, keep them keen.

It's not even funny to be honest because some of these women end up in abusive relationships.

If you're seriously unhappy in a relationship, my advice is to leave.

A lot of these women will not leave an abusive guy for love nor money. Some of them may complain about him, but others will defend him with all their might, even while they're wearing sunglasses in the middle of winter to hide the black eye the same man they're defending gave them.

In fact, it can be many years and a few babies later before these women finally gather up the courage to leave. Some of them only leave to go back or to find another Bad Boy to abuse them in one way or another. While others leave and mean it. They end up on the run in women's refuges watching their backs when they go to visit someone that their abusive ex knows the whereabouts of.

All because they didn't want to be with a nice guy.

Some of these women give a nice guy a shot, but then they end up being a bitch to him. They walk all over him, metaphorically and literally. He's usually too nice to leave so eventually she'll dump him or cheat on him with a Bad Boy.

You already know where that story ends.

Are You Deaf?

In general, men say similar stuff to what I am saying in this book. There's no beating around the bush. I say what I mean and I mean what I say. I don't necessarily sugar coat my words, although believe it or not, a lot of the time I do. The most important thing for me is to say my words nice and clear so everyone can understand.

The problem with that is a lot of women tend to read into things.

A lot.

You may not realise that she's paying attention to your every word, tone of voice etc. but she is. Especially as women are masters of multitasking. They'll seem like they're not listening because they're doing other stuff simultaneously, but they are. They'll still be listening, noting everything a man says.

Every little thing you say can be analysed, re-analysed and discussed with her friends for more analysis later.

Women tend to read more into what we say. They'll be thinking: What did he mean when he said that? Unfortunately for them, they don't seem to understand there is no hidden meaning behind our words. We don't speak in riddles like women tend to. We mean what we say when we say it. Otherwise, we would have said something different.

There's no reason to add meaning to what a man says because men do one of two things.

They either speak their minds clearly so there's no ambiguity, or they can't find the words to express themselves, they don't feel comfortable expressing themselves or haven't thought things over enough in their minds; which all leads to them saying nothing.

Men either say what they mean or say nothing at all.

There's not usually an in-between. It's black or white. Words or no words. If we don't say any words, just wait. Not with a stopwatch and your hand on your hip telling us you're waiting. It may actually take a little while. Maybe minutes, hours, sometimes days.

We men like to mull things over in our minds.

When we eventually express ourselves, we will say what we mean. Nothing more, nothing less. There's no need to take notes and go and consult your friends to try to find out the true meaning behind our words.

We've already done all the filtering, that's why sometimes we take so long.

Women will go over things in their mind to try to find answers to questions that don't really exist. Their lack of ability to make up their minds will lead them to consult their mafia of friends for further opinions on what their man has said.

A man will tell them 'A' but they will come out with 'XYZ' possibilities of the true meaning of 'A'. This isn't algebra. 'A' means 'A'. It's as simple as that.

The fact that women do this frustrates men worldwide. We start to think that this woman must be deaf or something. I just said 'A', but now she's quoting me as saying 'XY and Z'.

Was I not clear enough in my words?

This will lead to men repeating themselves, which is the best thing to do in my opinion, or saying the same thing in a different way, which is the worst thing to do because she'll go back to the lab for analysis because it now sounds different.

I think the best way to spell things out is to provide clear examples so that people can see what you're saying and experience it through a storyline. It tends to make things clear. That's actually some advice to both sexes.

My advice to women is to listen carefully and don't go turning what a man said into something different. Take it as it is.

Simple.

The Real Problem Is

Women endure a lot throughout their lives. From the moment their menstrual cycle starts, it's usually the source of monthly pain or a feeling of constant uncomfortability, year in year out.

Even when they become pregnant, the pain previously felt gets replaced with worrying uncertainty about their changing bodies. They may suffer a miscarriage, which is obviously upsetting for both parents, but it's even more heart-breaking for a woman.

They may suffer from morning sickness, as well as all the aches and pains that occupy her body during pregnancy. The ever fluctuating hormones that change her mood, the increasing need to go toilet, alongside having crazy cravings for strange food combinations at the most random of times.

Her size will grow, which may give them doubts of whether they will be able to get back to a size she feels comfortable with, along with the worries about stretchmarks.

Then, there's the sheer weight they have to carry around that causes back problems. There's also the excruciating contractions that come with labour. The labour itself can last several hours, and, despite the wealth of pain relief available, it can still be a terrifying experience.

And, the birth is only the beginning of her life metamorphosis. There's also the matter of breastfeeding, which can lead to sore nipples or the baby not taking to the breast, which then incites worries about the child's health. Of course, there's looking after the child for the next 18 years, plus any other children that come into the equation.

Whether she has children or not, she'll have the menopause to look forward to, with a sure delivery of hot and cold flushes when she least expects it. And, that's not the half of it. There's a wealth of different symptoms depending on the woman, none of them particularly pleasant.

With all the hormones rushing through a woman and all the strains put upon them throughout their lives, it's no wonder that they have problems that affect the men around them.

The problem with women is, despite all their faults and issues; their wild mood swings, their ultra-sensitiveness, their insecurities, their possessiveness, their Jekyll and Hyde personalities, their inability to make up their minds or even speak their minds, we just can't live without them, literally.

Their beauty attracts us, their voices arouse us, their softness embraces us, their warmth melts us and their vulnerabilities make us want to protect them.

Their strange way of doing things keeps us men intrigued to find out more about them. They drive us crazy and we most probably drive them crazy too. But we can't keep away from them.

We are pulled into their orbit hopelessly.

We'll see an attractive woman and all of a sudden we can't stop staring. Our eyes are transfixed on her every move. We'll admire her beauty, waiting for her gaze to meet ours. Looking for a little smile or some sort of sign to indicate that they're interested. We'll approach her and make some small talk.

Because we want her.

Men love women.

We'll do silly things to try to catch a woman's attention.

Throughout the animal kingdom, animals have all sorts of mating calls. We humans aren't any different. Many of the things men do are to impress women, whether consciously or unconsciously. The way we dress, the clothes we buy, the cars we drive, the way we converse, the way we act. A lot of it is to attract the opposite sex.

How many asexual men do you know?

I don't know any personally.

All the heterosexual men I know, are always talking about women. Either a current woman in their life, an ex that they can't stop complaining about or longing for, or one they are interested in that they have yet to capture.

The fact is that women are central to our lives. A lot of the time we are thinking about them, talking about them or talking to them. Trying to get their attention. Trying to impress them. Trying to stand out from the other men in the world.

We want to be special to a woman and we want to find that special someone. Even if we don't want to admit it. Even if we don't even realise it. Some men are dogs, so they try to impress multiple women at once, but it's the same thing, just multiplied.

So the real problem is, you woman are so annoying that we men just can't keep away!